LEMURS

and Other Animals of the Madagascar Rain Forest

by James Martin

Photographs by the Author

Reading consultant:

John Manning, Professor of Reading, University of Minnesota

Capstone Press

MINNEAPOLIS

Printed in the United States of America.

Capstone Press • 2440 Fernbrook Lane • Minneapolis, MN 55447

Editorial Director   John Coughlan
Managing Editor   John Martin
Copy Editor   Gil Chandler

Library of Congress Cataloging-in-Publication Data

Martin, James, 1950-
   Lemurs and other animals of the Madagascar rain forest /
   by James Martin.
      p. cm.
   Includes bibliographical references and index.
   ISBN 1-56065-237-3
   1. Lemurs--Madagascar--Juvenile literature. 2. Rain
forest fauna--Madagascar--Juvenile literature. [1. Lemurs
2. Rain forest animals. 3. Zoology--Madagascar.]
I. Title.
QL737.P95M385   1995
599.8'1--dc20   94-22824
                                CIP
                                AC

ISBN: 1-56065-237-3

99 98 97 96 95   8 7 6 5 4 3 2 1

Table of Contents

Range Map 4

Facts about Lemurs 5

Chapter 1 What is a Primate? 7

Chapter 2 The Island of Madagascar........... 11

Chapter 3 Early Animals of Madagascar 15

Chapter 4 Indri, Ringtail and
Sifaka Lemurs 19

Chapter 5 Creatures of the Spiny Forest 27

Chapter 6 Aye Aye, Bamboo, and
Mouse Lemurs.......................... 31

Chapter 7 Other Living Things on
Madagascar 37

Chapter 8 The Endangered Environment
of the Lemur............................. 42

Glossary...................................... 45

To Learn More 46

Some Useful Addresses 47

Index... 48

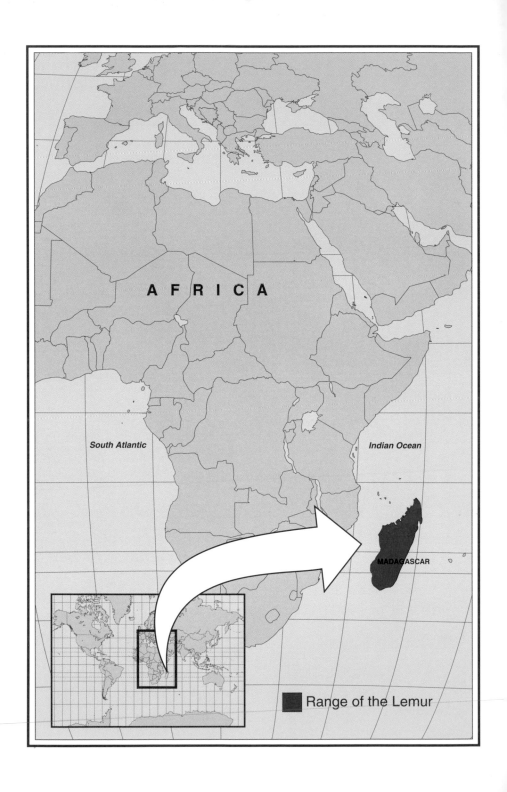

A F R I C A

South Atlantic

Indian Ocean

MADAGASCAR

Range of the Lemur

Facts about Lemurs

Scientific Names: *Lemuridae* (ringtail lemurs), *Cheirogaleidae* (mouse lemurs), *Indriidae* (indri and sifaka lemurs), and *Daubentoniidae* (aye-ayes).

Description: Squirrel- to cat-size primates.

Length: Mouse lemurs grow to only 5 inches (13 centimeters) with 6-inch (15.5-centimeter) tails. Indri lemurs may reach 3 feet (1 meter) with small 2-inch (5-centimeter) tails.

Weight: Full-grown male indris may weigh more than 15 pounds (6.8 kilograms). The largest mouse lemurs weigh only 2.5 ounces (.7 kilograms).

Color: Often brightly colored.

Distinctive Habits: Most lemurs spend their time in trees gathering food. Ringtails, however, spend most of their time on the ground. Most lemurs are also active mainly at night.

Food: Lemurs are mainly vegetarian, eating only leaves, fruit, and bark. However, some also eat insects.

Reproductive cycle: Most lemurs mate between April and June. The female gives birth to a single offspring in the fall.

Life span: Unknown in the wild.

Habitat: Tropical forests.

Range: The island of Madagascar.

Chapter 1
What is a Primate?

Branches shake. White shapes jump from tree to tree like pinballs. When the jumping stops, wide-eyed faces look down. The faces belong to sifaka lemurs. These long-tailed creatures are related to monkeys, apes, and humans.

What is a Primate?
Both humans and lemurs are **primates**. Primates have unusually large brains. And their

teeth are multi-purpose–so they can eat both meat and plants.

Scientists divide primates into two groups. **Anthropoids** include monkeys, apes, and humans. **Prosimians** include lemurs.

Prosimians like lemurs were once thought to be primitive primates, without the intelligence or the ability to live in groups that the anthropoids had. We now know that lemurs have as much intelligence as monkeys.

The hand of a lemur resembles our own. Like us, lemurs have fingerprints, fingernails, and a thumb that allows them to grasp things.

Lemurs' eyes, like ours, look straight ahead. This gives them the **depth perception** needed for life in the forest. Like humans, lemurs have large brains. Also, like us, lemurs are curious–and very careful when something new appears in the forest.

Chapter 2

The Island of Madagascar

Lemurs live only in Madagascar, a large island near Africa. Millions of years ago, lemurs migrated to the island from the African continent. That was before the island had drifted away from the mainland.

Madagascar is the fourth largest island in the world. It's about the size of Texas or Nova Scotia.

Humans first settled on Madagascar only 2,000 years ago. Because the languages spoken on Madagascar are like the languages

of Indonesia, scientists think that the first
settlers may have been Indonesian sailors
blown off course. Today, nearly 12 million
people live on the island.

The tropical plants and animals on
Madagascar are unlike any others in the world.
Lemurs live all over the island. Sifakas live in
a wet, narrow canyon on the western side of the
island. To the north and east, rain forests
contain many other types of lemurs, as well as
many strange insects and crocodiles. A forest
of **spiny** desert plants lies to the south. A high,
cool plateau sits in the center of the island, and
sand dunes, beaches, and mangrove trees line
the coast.

Chapter 2

Early Animals of Madagascar

The first lemurs appeared 65 million years ago, soon after dinosaurs became extinct. Lemurs once lived in the Americas and in Africa. But they eventually disappeared–except on Madagascar.

On Madagascar lemurs were safe. There were no large predators or deadly snakes. Lemurs didn't need to fight monkeys for food and places to live. The most dangerous hunters, humans, didn't come to the island until 2,000 years ago.

The macaco lemur

Early Lemurs: Megalapadis and Tratratratra

The first human settlers on Madagascar found an even stranger wildlife than we know today. One early lemur, Megalapadis, was the size of a gorilla.

The giant Megalapadis was not hostile to humans. With no natural enemies there was no reason for it to learn how to fight. Humans, however, quickly slaughtered it.

Another large early lemur was the 200-pound (90-kilogram) Tratratratra, which disappeared 300 years ago.

The Madagascar Elephant Bird

The Madagascar elephant bird was the largest bird in the world, growing 10 feet (three meters) high and laying eggs up to three feet (one meter) across. A single egg from the elephant bird could make a two-gallon (7.57-liter) omelette. Unhatched eggs are still found on the island.

Like the Megalapadis, the elephant bird disappeared shortly after humans discovered the island. The elephant bird, which could not fly, made an easy target for hunters. The last elephant bird died 500 years ago.

Chapter 3

Indri, Ringtail, and Sifaka Lemurs

The indri is the largest lemur remaining to this day. It grows to three feet (one meter) tall. It is the only lemur without a tail. Despite its size, it can jump with great skill. But if it is caught and kept in a cage, the indri will not survive.

Indri live in groups in pockets of Madagascar's thick rain forest. If people cut down much more of the island's rain forest, however, the indri will also vanish.

The sifaka lemur

Ringtail Lemurs and Sifaka Lemurs

Ringtail and sifaka lemurs live in family groups in the trees lining the southern rivers of Madagascar. They spend the days searching for food or shelter from the sun. At night they sleep high in the **canopy**–the upper branches of the rain forest trees.

Female Leaders

Females lead the family groups. The mothers get the best food. And they decide when the group should move from one tree to another.

Males often move from one group to another. They mate with females from different groups.

Moving Around

For sifakas, moving on the ground is dangerous. The lemur leader always takes her time at the edge of a clearing before following

The ring-tailed lemur

a path. An eagle or a *kite*–a kind of vulture–can easily kill a sifaka in an open area. The lemur isn't able to hide among the branches or jump to safety if attacked.

Because their feet are built for holding on to branches, sifakas don't walk. Instead, they skip sideways across the ground, the same way they leap from branch to branch. At a distance they look like bouncing tennis balls.

Staying on the Ground

Ringtail lemurs, however, prefer travelling on the ground. Groups of 12 to 25 lemurs patrol their territory with ringed tails held high. In low brush, only the tails are visible. It looks like a group of strange periscopes.

Snorting and Stink-Fighting

Ringtail lemurs are the most sociable lemurs. They spend hours grooming one another and caring for their young. On summer

It is safer for the sifaka lemur to leap from branch to branch than to walk.

afternoons, they escape the heat of the high branches by lying on the cool ground. When alert, they snort as if clearing their throats.

In mating season, male ringtails become aggressive. They shout and threaten one another. When they're angry, they fight or use their tails to throw a smelly liquid at their opponents. The stink fights stop and the males calm down when mating season ends.

Creatures of the Spiny Forest

In Madagascar's dry spiny forest, sharp barbs cover most of the desert plants there. Small gourds with thorny **shoots** hug the ground. Long branches of the octopus tree, with tiny round leaves, wave in the breeze. Giant plants that look like cactus offer some shade from the burning sun.

Sifaka lemurs and ringtail lemurs leap from plant to plant without hurting their soft hands. They nibble on the greenery, taking care to avoid the sharp parts.

Chapter 4

Creatures of
the Spiny Forest

Lepilemurs

Unlike sifakas and ringtails, the small lepilemurs move about the spiny forest at night. They sleep in the hollows of octopus trees and dine on the plant's tiny leaves.

As darkness falls, lepilemurs fill the forest with their chatter. Although they can leap great distances, they don't travel far from

Lepilemurs sleep in the hollows of trees.

home. A lepilemur's territory is only about 65 feet (20 meters) across.

The Strange Diet of Lepilemurs

Lepilemurs eat leaves, which are hard to digest because of their **cellulose**. Many animals that eat a steady diet of cellulose–like cows–have several stomachs. Others have extra-large stomachs that hold a large number of **bacteria**. Bacteria help to digest the cellulose. Lepilemurs have bacteria-rich **digestive systems**, but small stomachs. To give their stomachs a second chance to digest their food, they re-eat their own **droppings**.

The lemur's food supply is in great danger. People are destroying the spiny forests. They burn the plants for fuel and clear land for crops. Cactus is taking over, and only small pockets of spiny forest remain.

The lepilemur shares the spiny forest with the endangered radiated tortoise *(right).*

Chapter 5

Aye-aye, Bamboo, and Mouse Lemurs

Unusual animals can survive on islands. There is less competition for food than on the mainland.

Lemurs and other strange species would probably have died out on the mainland. They thrive today on the island of Madagascar.

The Aye-aye Lemur

The aye-aye looks like a lemur who has stuck its finger in a light socket. Its sparse,

The mouse lemur *(left)* is the world's smallest primate.

frizzy hair points straight out. Its huge eyes have a startled look. Bat-like ears stick out to the sides and swing back and forth. Its front teeth look like a beaver's. Long, black fingers spread out from a bony hand.

For years scientists argued over whether it was a true lemur. Studies eventually proved that it was.

The Aye-aye's Ears and Long Third Finger

The aye-aye's ears and long third finger help it to hunt. The ears move around and try to catch the sound of tiny beetles chewing under the tree bark. As it listens, the aye-aye taps on the tree with its third finger. This may cause the beetles to move and reveal their location. The aye-aye also listens for hollow spots beetles have created in the tree.

When the aye-aye hears the beetles, it rips the bark away with its sharp front teeth. It spears the beetles with the sharp nail of its third finger. Then it eats the wiggling insects.

The aye-aye lemur

The third finger also comes in handy for eating nuts. The aye-aye carves a hole in the nut's shell with its front teeth and then scoops out the meat of the nut with its finger. It also uses the finger to collect sap from trees.

Living Alone in the Dark

Aye-ayes live alone in the dark. They do not live in groups. A meeting between two aye-ayes usually leads to a fight.

Villagers believe that seeing an aye-aye is bad luck. For this reason, many native people kill aye-ayes on sight.

Scientists once thought the aye-aye was the rarest and most nearly extinct of lemurs. But this lemur's secretive ways hid its true numbers. Aye-ayes may survive, even if other lemurs become extinct.

Bamboo Lemurs

Bamboo lemurs live in the deep jungle. They are named after the bamboo plant. These lemurs eat only the shoots, **pith**, and base of this plant–not the leaves.

A Poisonous Diet

The golden bamboo lemur, a variety not discovered until 1985, eats bamboo leaves. These are full of poisonous **cyanide**. Every day it eats enough cyanide to kill five other lemurs. Golden bamboo lemurs are somehow **immune** to the poison.

The Mouse Lemur

The mouse lemur is the world's smallest primate. Only five inches (13 centimeters) long, they are the lemurs safest from extinction. They can survive in small corners of the forest. In that way they remain unharmed by humans.

Although tiny, mouse lemurs are great leapers. A five-inch (13-centimeter) mouse lemur can jump 10 feet (three meters). That's 24 times the length of its body. To equal that feat, a six-foot (1.8-meter) human would have to jump 120 feet (37 meters).

Marking Territory

Mouse lemurs mark their territory by **urinating** into their cupped hands and spreading the urine on their feet. They then wipe their hands and feet on branches, leaving a smelly trail.

During the day, groups of mouse lemurs sleep in leafy nests or in hollow trees. They feed on flowers and fruit. They will eat insects, too.

Chapter 6

Other Living Things on Madagascar

Many other strange animals inhabit the forests of Madagascar. There are odd reptiles, **mammals**, insects, and plants living all over the island.

Geckos

Leaf-tailed geckos cling to tree trunks and watch for insects. The skin of the gecko changes color to match the pattern of **lichen** and bark on the tree. The gecko sits with its head down. When its insect lunch passes by, it leaps into the air and catches the prey in its mouth.

Chameleons

Most of the world's true chameleons live on Madagascar. The smallest are only two inches (five centimeters) long. The largest grow to three feet (.9 meter). They hide among dead leaves on the forest floor. They keep watch with two eyes that move in different directions.

A chameleon traps bugs with a tongue that is longer than its body. The tongue slips over a tapered bone in its mouth–like a swordholder over a sword. When the tongue contracts on the bone, it quickly slides forward. The only time a chameleon's eyes look in the same direction is when it shoots its tongue.

Chameleons change color to communicate with other chameleons. When one chameleon invades another's territory, both adopt warning colors. These colors are usually much brighter than their normal green or brown.

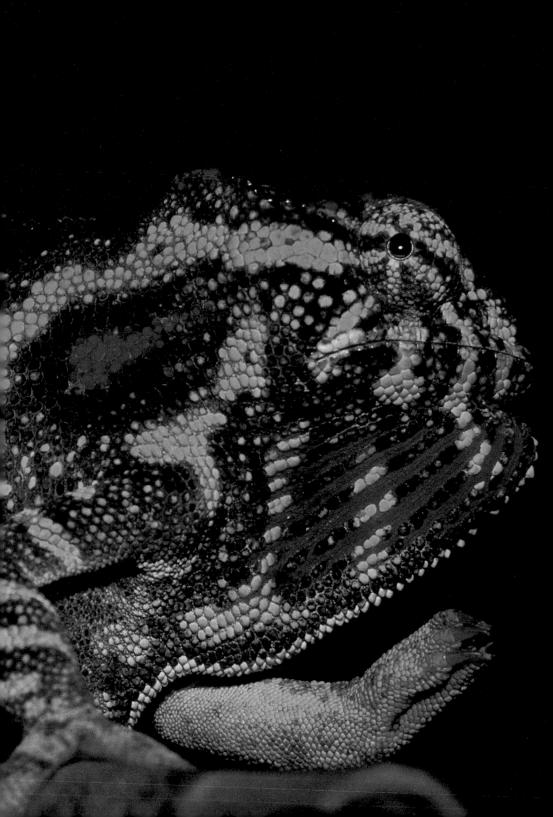

Chameleons also change their color to change their body temperature. A cold chameleon can warm itself by turning dark on the side facing the sun.

The Radiated Tortoise

The radiated tortoise is one of the rarest animals on earth. It lives in the spiny forest, where it munches on the pulpy plants. A tortoise can live longer than a human being.

But the number of radiated tortoises is falling. Much of their forest home has been destroyed by farmers. Also, many tortoises are caught and sent to be sold as pets in shops around the world.

Insect Mimics

Some of the insect world's best **mimics** live in the rain forest of Madagascar. One looks like a walking leaf.

The insects of another group are named "walking sticks." Except for tiny wings, they look just like twigs.

Flatworms and Leeches

Bright orange, two-headed flatworms also inhabit the rain forest of Madagascar. They are about seven inches (17.5 centimeters) long. They move across rotting plants, walking on both ends of their bodies.

The rain forest is also home to unusual leeches. They drop from wet leaves to painlessly suck blood from their animal victims. They fill themselves with blood, growing to look like ugly water balloons. Then they drop off.

Tenrecs

Tenrecs are rat-sized porcupines that live in burrows in the rain forest. Many scientitsts think the first mammals looked something like tenrecs.

The Fossa

The fossa (pronounced "foosh") is the largest predator on Madagascar. It is a **civet**, a cat-like animal that hunts all over the island. Because fossa move only at night, few people sce them. Sleeping lemurs must keep alert to avoid becoming the dinner of a fossa.

Chapter 7

The Endangered Environment of the Lemur

The environment of Madagascar is in great danger. Humans have destroyed the forests, wiped out animal life, and damaged the soil.

The rivers of Madagascar run red with dirt. From space, astronauts can see streaks of red from the island's rivers running into the sea. They say it looks like the island is bleeding.

Here's why the rivers are red. The people of the rain forest live on rice. In order to grow rice they clear the land by burning the forest. They sell the burned trees as charcoal for fuel. Each tree only brings a dollar or two.

A dirt-filled stream in Madagascar

Farmers then plant rice without making **terraces**. When heavy rains come, the soil washes away. The farmers then move to a new area, and the cycle of destruction begins again.

When there were few people living on Madagascar, the forest could recover easily. Today the population of the island is double what it was 30 years ago. This puts pressure on the farmers to grow more rice.

As the forest burns and soil washes down the rivers, farmers are running out of land. Topsoil for growing crops can take millions of years to form. Without forest and without soil, the people of Madagascar will starve.

The people of Madagascar are plundering the animal and plant life of their island. They capture chameleons and other reptiles for sale as pets. None of these will ever reproduce in the wild again.

Only an international effort can stop the final destruction of the Madagascar rain forest, the home of the lemur. Private organizations do what they can. Foreign governments have contributed some money. Without massive assistance, however, lemurs and the other wonders of the Madagascar rain forest will soon vanish. Forever.

Glossary

anthropoids–a group of primates; includes monkeys, apes, and humans

bacteria–tiny single-celled animals

canopy–the uppermost branches of a rain forest

cellulose–a very tough substance found in plants

civet–a flesh-eating, catlike animal found in Africa and Asia

cyanide–a deadly poison found in bamboo leaves

depth perception–the ability to see objects that are far away

digestive system–a group of organs which help the body use food

droppings–the dung of animals

immune–to be safe from disease or poison

lichen–a moss-like plant

mammal–a group of animals with fur on their bodies. Female mammals' bodies also produce milk which they feed to their young.

mimic–to copy

pith–the soft inner part of a plant

primate–a member of the group of mammals which includes lemurs, monkeys, apes, and humans

prosimians–a group of primates which includes lemurs

shoot–a small plant

spiny–having sharp, pointed needles

terrace–a flat section of earth built onto a hill

urinate–to rid liquid waste from the body

To Learn More

Anderson, Norman D. and Walter R. Brown. *Lemurs.* New York: Dodd, Mead, 1984.

Aldis, Rodney. *Rainforests.* New York: Dillon, 1991.

George, Michael. *Rain Forest.* Mankato, MN: Creative Education, 1992.

Hamilton, Jean. *Tropical Rainforests.* San Luis Obispo, CA: Blake, 1990.

Jennings, Terry L. *Tropical Forests.* Freeport, NY: M. Cavendish, 1987.

Landau, Elaine. *Tropical Rain Forests Around the World.* New York: F. Watts, 1990.

Carpenter, Allan and Matthew Maginnis. *Malagasy Republic (Madagascar).* Chicago: Childrens Press, 1972

Madagascar in Pictures. Minneapolis: Lerner Publications, 1988.

D'Amato, Janet and Alex D'Amato. *African Animals through African Eyes.* New York: J. Messner, 1971.

Montroll, John. *African Animals in Origami.* New York: Dover, 1991.

Some Useful Addresses

African Wildlife Foundation
1717 Massachusetts Avenue, N.W., Suite 602
Washington, DC 20036

Conservation International
1015 18th St. N.W., Suite 1000
Washington, DC 20036

Friends of the Earth
218 D St. S.E.
Washington, DC 20003

Friends of the Earth/Les Ami(e)s de la terre
215 Laurier Ave., #701
Ottawa ON K1P 5J6

Rainforest Action Network
450 Sansome, Suite 700
San Francisco, CA 94111

Rainforest Alliance
270 Lafayette Street, Suite 512
New York, NY 10012

World Wildlife Fund
1250 24th Strect, N.W.
Washington, DC 20037

Index

Africa, 11
anthropoids, 8
apes, 7
aye-ayes, 5, 31-34

bacteria, 28
bamboo leaves, 34
bamboo lemurs, 34
brains, 7-8

cactus, 28
canopy, 20
cellulose, 28
chameleons, 38, 40, 44
charcoal, 42
colors, 5, 38, 40
crocodiles, 13
cyanide, 34
depth perception, 8
digestive systems, 28
dinosaurs, 15

eagles, 22
elephant bird, 17
environment, 42

fighting, 25, 33
flatworms, 41
food, 5, 8, 20, 27-28, 32-35, 40

fossa, 41

geckos, 37-38
gorillas, 17
gourds, 25

habitat, 5
hands, 8
humans, 7-8, 11, 15, 17, 19, 28, 34-35, 40, 42-44

Indonesia, 13
indri lemurs, 5, 19

kites, 22

leeches, 41
length, 5
lepilemurs, 27-28
lichen, 37
life span, 5

Madagascar, 5, 11, 15, 17, 19-20, 25, 31, 37-38, 40-44
megalapadis, 17
monkeys, 7-8, 15
mouse lemurs, 5, 35

Nova Scotia, 11

octopus trees, 25, 27

offspring, 5, 22

primates, 7-8, 35
prosimians, 8

radiated tortoise, 40
range, 5
reproduction, 5, 20, 25
ringtail lemurs, 5, 20, 22, 25, 27
rivers, 42

scientific names, 5
scientists, 13, 32, 34, 41
sifaka lemurs, 5, 7, 13, 20, 22, 25, 27

teeth, 8, 32
tenrecs, 41
terraces, 43
Texas, 11
thumbs, 8
tratratratra, 17

walking sticks, 40
weight, 5